Les Fièvres

et les

Humeurs

St. Expedite Press Presents

Les Fièvres

et les

Humeurs

Three Themes in Chamber Verse

Christopher Sandbatch

St. Expedite Press
Nouvelle-Orléans

First edition.
Printed in the United States of America.

Published by St. Expedite Press
New Orleans, Louisiana
www.stexpedite.press

ISBN: 979-8-9942035-0-7

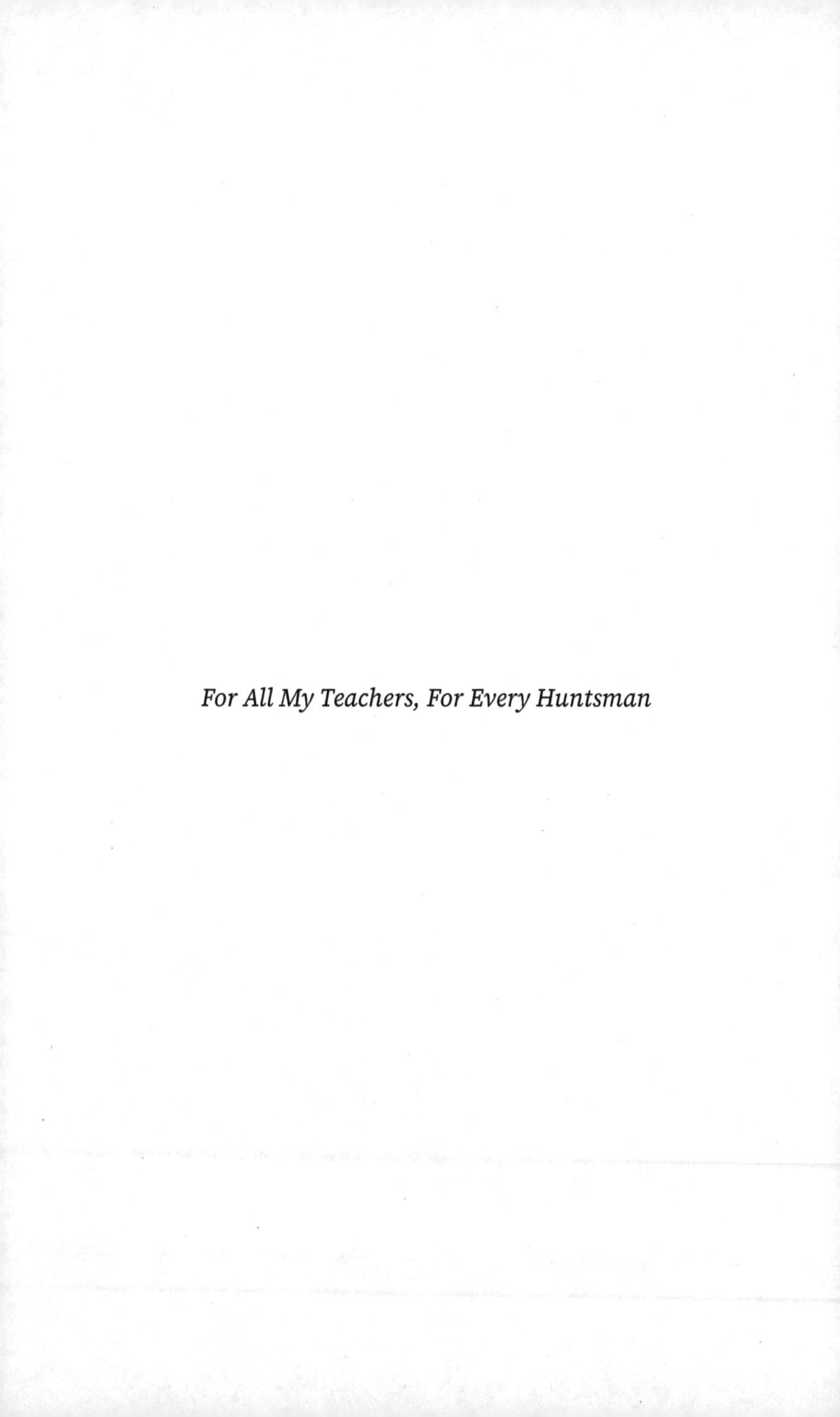

For All My Teachers, For Every Huntsman

Night

My voice for you; so gentle, so exhausted
Bestirs nocturnal silence, deep and frosted.
Beside my bed a melancholy flame
Burns on; my verses merge, descend, the same
As little streams of love, all fed by you.
Within the dark your eyes still strike me through,
They shine, they lean toward mine; I hear your breath
My friend, my tenderest friend... I love you...

Odessa
26 April, 1823
— Alexander Pushkin

Programme

Preface

Certain emotional states command recurrence; others collapse at their moment of instance. From others still, we can manage little more than a disciplined withdrawal. What emerged from this second book (but where is the first?) was not a sequence of lyrical sallies but the architecture of an emotional arc. That is, three movements governed less by object than by the inescapability of the subjective "quest".

The organizing terms—*Obsession, Ruin, Désir*—are therefore not psychological states so much as climates of tonality. Obsession is treated as a formal problem: repetition, fixation, excess of return. Ruin is not aftermath but atmosphere: the condition in which ethical and aesthetic structures decay at different speeds. Desire, finally, appears not as appetite but as residue; the irradiated substance remaining after fixation and collapse have exhausted themselves.

What does that remainder look like? My answer, and the answer I submit here, is *music*. I have come to think of poems, especially in sequence, as inhabiting keys rather than themes. A key does not dictate content; it establishes gravity. It determines what kinds of motion feel natural, what kinds of resolution feel false, what gestures must be repeated until they either break or transfigure.

In this sense, tonality becomes a discipline rather than a metaphor—a way of preventing mere intensity from mistaking itself for meaning.

Tonality, as I use it here, is not nostalgia for harmony but a refusal of arbitrariness. Key supplies orientation without promising resolution. It permits dissonance, even insists upon it, but denies dissonance the privilege of pretending to be depth on its own. Under tonal constraint, excess must justify itself; repetition must prove endurance; collapse must leave a paw print worth tracking.

To score a book in this way is to betray belief that tonal coherence still matters. It may seem antiquated, even reactionary. That charge I accept, but these poems confess nothing.

L'Obsession

Op. II

Solo Cantata in A Major

Very early in my life it was too late. It was already too late when I was eighteen. Obsession was already there.

— Marguerite Duras

Apologia

So what is obsession? Let me show you. Obsession starts without hope. It's born in strange places & sideways looks in public places. Obsession starts in a conversation with someone you maybe just thought you wanted to fuck.

Obsession starts without hope.

I've fallen back on form here because obsession has form. Every work of art is an uncommitted crime, and every artist is a kind of criminal, driven by an obsession with what he alone sees.

Obsession— it has form until it doesn't. It is a fixation. A line or an idea that enters your mind once and either flows back out or sticks but either way it comes howling back in; there's nothing you can do.

Obsession has shape & if it has shape it has form here is the form.

We Tell Ourselves Stories

What's funny is we really do say I love you
  as goodbye in Los Angeles. You were dressed
in nothing but a tan line and one shoe.

I watched your ankle flex. You sort of confessed
  you'd slept with someone else last week, or not
the past was traffic, and you weren't impressed.

Your toes were blistered from the heat. I thought
  they looked like grapes embalmed in reddish paint.
You let me touch you, then said, *Please don't get caught.*

The ceiling fan revolved, deliberate and faint.
  You fixed your gaze on the vent's dull brass
reflected once, then gone. A kind of saint?

I flipped a quarter and it landed on your ass.
I love you is how you say goodbye in Cyberspace,
  too.

Quartet For Two

(Do You Want to Get the Girl?)

"Dude, four people are involved,"
says someone else.

Standing plain: the real girl
sharpens the scene.
Suddenly attentive to real stakes,
it feels like I'm the one being hunted now.

Still the real girl,
standing where my thought curdles
itself into something solid.

Brightens, suddenly more knowable,
I catch myself watching, slightly misgiven,
soften into innocence. Performative.
No one is doing harm.

My friend names them back:
"one who is only geometry,
the real one, the imagined one,"
as though speaking her reframes
the frame.

Washed-out morning, spared from scrutiny.
Still real, I watch while wanting
to be without; wanting.

Real. I wish she constructed
me, real, and from a voice inside.

Unadorned again. Returning, smaller,
almost nonimagined, spotted.
Angled. "Stand a little closer, please."

Her frame now looks back at me.
A quartet after all.

Variations on a Natural Woman

(Roundel Mutations, an interlude in B Flat Minor)

I: Andante con Moto

And what would you do, seeing me stare
At your calves, blanketed lightly in hair
Oh, sunlight entwined in the rivers soft bend,
Where narrow the streets and the levee roads end.
I've drunk all my wine, with nothing to spare
But what would you do, seeing me stare?

Some lace on the sill, and the musk of old rooms,
A spring twig of longing under lemon-tree blooms.
It is nothing, you say, just a street in the sun,
But your calves in the daylight, the way that you run
I will think of the salt on your skin and your care.
But what would you do, seeing me stare?

II: Con Nebbia

(With Mist/Static)

And what would you do, seeing me stare
at your calves, blanketed lightly (yes, really) in hair
Oh, sunlight entwined, Oh static in the riverbend
where the phones don't ring and levee roads end.
I've drunk all my wine with nothing to share,
but what would you do, seeing me stare?

Some lace on the sill radio hiss, the damp of old rooms
a flutter (it skips) of longing in lemon-tree blooms.
It is nothing, you say, just a street in the sun,
but your calves in the daylight (the way you run)
I will think of the salt on your skin, your disordered care.
And what would you do, seeing me stare?

III: Capriccioso, dissoluto

And what would you do, seeing me stare
at your calves, blanketed lightly unshaven & bare
Touched by the day. Sunlight, river-bend,
narrow streets, where levee roads end.
I've drunk all my wine (left my glass there)
But what would you do,
if you saw me stare?

Some lace on the sill, and musk slathered rooms
(a scent I keep finding in afternoon gloom).
You say it is nothing a street, some sun
But your calves in the daylight, they blur as you run
I'll remember the salt on your skin, the ick in your glare.
Does it bother you? This?
That I'm losing my hair?

IV: Sognante

(Dreamlike)

And what would you do
  seeing me stare
at your calves unshaven wild
  light gilding the hair
(sun spooled in the river's bend,
  where narrow streets lean,
levee roads end).
  I've drunk all my wine
with nothing to spare
  but what would you do,
seeing me stare?

  Some lace, a crooked sill
the stink of old rooms
  snaked into you,
a twinkle of longing,
  & lemon-tree blooms
It is nothing, you say,
  just a street in the sun,
but the shock of your calves!
  my heart flutters and runs
But I'll think of the salt
  on your skin, your careless air.
I wish you'd come over!
  and be my fine mare...

V: Da Capo

(Return)

And what would you do,
  seeing me stare
At your calves,
  blanketed lightly in hair?
Oh, sunlight entwined
  in the river's soft bend,
Where narrow the streets
  and the levee roads end.
I've drunk all my wine,
  with nothing to spare
But what would you do,
  seeing me stare?

Some lace on the sill,
  and the musky old rooms,
A flicker of longing
  in lemon-tree blooms.
It is nothing, you say,
  just a street in the sun,
But your calves in the daylight,
  the way that you run
I will think of the salt
  on your skin and I care.
Just what you would do,
  seeing me stare?

VI: Scherzo alla Shatter

And what would you do, seeing me stare
  At your calves covered, golden, frankly in hair,
catching the last of the Bywater light,
  Rays drifting sideways, just beyond riversight.
I've drunk all my wine (left the bottle somewhere)
  but what are you doing, watching me stare?

Still lace on the sill, the musk of old rooms
  Our shimmery static, in lemon-tree blooms.
It is nothing, you say, just a street just the sun
  but your calves, in that light on the run
I will taste of the salt, & bend you over my chair!
  Now what will you do?

  You know I'm standing there?
  I'll just be right there...

Erato

Chrysanthemum stroke.
Blossom / vanish / reappear.

Bloodless & baroque
Sidewinder Annunciation.
Never walking folding space.

A slant arrival.
You quiet rival.
Intention curves sideways.
Shatters distance.

One place, then another.
Layered lacquered silk lifting
buries you inside the fold.

Never carried.
Never beckoned.
There then
There again.

Let the Flower Bleed

Thundering witness, paradise plume,
From the cracks in the ancient pavement you bloom,
Last night's lipstick, and gin on your breath.

Neighbors are whispering under the moon
Your slips at your ankles, you're mocking the priest.
Thundering witness, paradise plume.

Once you wore white, now you haunt every room,
Perfume of wild nights and broken bequests,
From the cracks in the ancient pavement you bloom.

Who counted the lovers you lost before noon?
Who kissed you in rain while the city confessed?
Thundering witness, paradise plume.

Petals rain gently, announcing your doom
You laugh at the ruin, you dare what is left.
From the cracks in the ancient pavement you bloom.

Scandalous beauty, obscene as a wound
Your dance in the heat, in the dress you undress.
Thundering witness, paradise plume,
From the cracks in the ancient pavement you bloom.

Rotflower, Rotflower

Rotflower, rotflower, come you to me.
Come broke, come bitch-hewn, come painted to be
The saints in my the window, there's drink in the drawer.
I want the perfume of a body gone sore.

Breathe me your breath like a funeral bell,
your hips like prophecy, dressed up for hell.
The girls in the hallway are starting to scream
your smile's my ruin, you fuck like a dream.

Rotflower, rotflower, teeth in your stem.
I ate all your scars and I savored them.
The plaster is cracking, the altar is wet.
Your tanline a dare I won't forget.

Come dirty, come eaten, come dragging the sea.
Roll on your latex, and come dance with me.
I devoured your name, & I begged for the more
I want our bodies to entwine at the core.

Rotflower, rotflower, bloom out of spite.
You bled on my chest and you came in the night.
There's saints in the windows who spit at the floor.
So leave them their heaven then give me some more.

Ruin

Op. III

Scena in E-flat Minor

Ruin is formal — Devil's work
Consecutive and slow —
Fail in an instant, no man did
Slipping — is Crashe's law —

— Emily Dickinson

Apologia

ruin is when you can't stop & can't go away / ruin is the mayor cutting a ribbon made of smoke / the senator calls it infrastructure & files a bill to rename the crater / the priest calls it providence / the banker calls it liquidity & sells futures to vegetarians / the general salutes a statue that has already excused its head

> children are dragging a lion skeleton down main street / while teachers pass out maps with no borders left / architects stare at blueprints full of holes & say symmetry is alive / & the parade keeps moving but the drummer has no drum & just bangs two broken doors together

ruin is not aftermath it is atmosphere / it is the reprise played before the song bends the steel / the orchestra tunes itself to fire alarms / alleys sing like choirs without throats / monuments erase their own obituaries / & everybody claps cause they got nothing left to drop

> the senator waves again: "look, progress!" / the cop pets his horse / the shopgirl sells souvenirs / the poet eats plaster & calls it sacrament / the child holds up a brick as if it were indeed a dove

ruin opens its mouth & lets them bricks fall out / crooked, burning / call it love if you must / call it ruin if you dare / call it nothing & still it will get tangled in your hair

ruin touches everything here is ruin

The Festival Is Over

Our city blazes. Hell ignites our night,
  Torch-shafts ascending, waltzing in the sky;
  Bronze windows flare; anonymous, the cry
Of revel bursts the pavements, harsh and white.

But fire feeds also itself. Towers must burn,
  Flay gay streamers; stuttering them to smoke.
  Blacken stone lions' cracking columns. Choke
On cinders, winds that wheel with each return.

Ash coils smiling up, scarifying stars,
  The alleys writhe, each mask dissolved, withdrawn;
  Gilt to black wick—the city's past now mars
Its own façade, and silence climbs the dawn.

Yet out of ruin, one keen ember gleams—
One will, a shard, surviving other dreams.

Broken Sonnet

(This Is Not A Sonnet)

We as one
Un ,un delay;
Each a blade,
Than could say.

For what we its due
In and will;
Desire ,and we knew
to law our fulfill.

Yet had we suffered little, little sense
Had reckoned out that adamant ire;
So—our armors broken, wrenched, and tense
We pressed as one along the blade of fire.

Thus am I driven: *Si fuerit amor*
Sicut amor tuus—who loves as you adore?

Not Orpheus, I

How does the city sit solitary, that was
  Full of people; widowed marble, pale with flame?
  Queen among harbors, empress of all shame,
Bride of the burnt, sovereign of our loss.

No lyre remains. Its thrones are charnel gold.
  Her dancers gone, the honeyed voices mute
  Only the wind's delirium through the chute
Of temples razed and columns numb with cold.

Not Orpheus, I—no backward-fixèd gaze,
  No lyrist's woe to petrify my feet.
Bearing no song for shadows nor sing praise;
  I gather up my remnant and retreat.

Let Orpheus linger, singing to the dust
Choose I the sea, the living, and the must.

Pushkin Takes Another Bow

Exiled!

Still I keep the Old Rite:
With spring's first blaze
Loose I a bird
into the air.

So small a mercy,
yet I feel it—
why curse God,
when I can grant
one creature
flight?

I am
open now
to consolation

God?
I will not rail
I have given
one living thing

Liberación(a)

We met where the border drips
   sweat into the armpit river.
Wild *María* with sulphur eyes,
   calico skirt & belt of twine
   laughing like a bullfighter banshee.

Her name in town was *Liberación(a).*
Three knives she had & brothers two—
   kept *dos pasos más* between her love & shoes.

She said, "Sleep is for the pig boys.
I dream in *rayo, loco de sol*
you dream in English, snowy & slow."

She called me *el extranjero*
   kicking dust on my hands.
I said, "loyal am I!
For you alone my midnights burn."

She spat: "*¿Te quiero?* Don't lie.
You'd church my body just to turn my color."

María dug a hole in my stare
   deep-drilled sighing smoke.

"*María, ¿estás desnuda?*" I said,
   but she kissed her fingers red
   threw a frog in the missionary's eye.

My leap-year heart given to her.
Her promises—ribbon slashes.

"*María, ¿por qué lloras?*" I said.
She laughed, "*Porque* I can't stop the frogs."
   Then vanished into the *arcaicos* of night.

White Boy

María
  who waits for you at home waits for very long
  damn how little we understand
  when we ride on your side of the sun.

Trying to dream in *rayo, loco de tanto sol*
  Cuando irrumpimos en el rostro del juicio.

This room gets hot early & faces the sun.
No one called all yesterday.

Finger to the window—morning creep—oil rainbow;
  dogs chase clouds down the street.

Luck's a witch, not a hare.
Door's open sun's up nobody watching.
Two clean shirts left. Wear a dirty one.

So if there's any softness in you?
Some turn of grace?
Some sly smile for me—give it now.

  Thin burn all the veils.

Snow Leopard, Memphis

Tail swish, brief as a wish.
Blur behind the painted boulder,
And two blue eyes, ancient and cool.

Fix me: stone, boy, and predator.
I stand—small, held by her hand
(My mother's brung me to the zoo.)

Ten feet apart: the spotted monarch,
Fur dusted with summer grit.
Breath steaming in the foreign heat.

What could I do, meeting such a gaze?
A rare thing.
Rare thing, indifferent queen,
Seeing through my heartbeat.

Some part of me thinks: let it take me,
Let myself be ended by that look—
(Rarity should outlast the common.)

We, believing ourselves special,
Should measure our lives
Against the gold
In those impossible eyes.

Impossible

You know, maybe
I've never met you,
Not even in a picture,
But right now you're a snow leopard—
Alone in the high blue cold,
Silent, moving where no one else will go.

You said it was impossible and snarled
A little, at the thought...

I don't know your real face,
But this one fits:
Wild, hidden,
Real as anything
I can say
Dream to hope
Hope to dream.

...So I thought I'd show you how
I make things real.

If anyone asks,
You're a snow leopard—
And I think, for now,
That's probably true.

And What Would You Do?

And what would you do, huh?—
  if I laid down in the dirt
    and opened my veins?—
      if I lit my coat on fire
      Watching your eyes reflect it?

You gonna judge me
  from your crackedice throne?

I buried my last kitten
  and never cried—
but here I am
  tearing at snow
    like it's an itching stye.

Think your silence makes you a saint?

Say something. To me.
Use them. Those teeth.

Then Into the High Place

I

The valley gapes, wind-shaken, wide–
Taking the upland trail, with need
And rifle, chimes the hunter's stride.
He climbs through mountain meadows, freed
By sunlight, spur, and broken reed,
Past limbs of trees and motes of dust;
The bloodless night begins to bleed–
He breathes the cold, accepts its trust.

What's left when hunger's bite is dulled?
He follows spoor, lets thoughts fall slack.
The mountain silence, wire-pulled,
Draws taut, then snaps behind his back–
Still upward, marked by ancient sign,
Those ember eyes that do not pine.

II

A stone upturned, a decade spent;
The snowline glittering, pawprint-faint—
He tracks by absentee intent
On costs that hunter, hunted paint.

What's measured here? What grace remains?
He stumbles on—a hunger sharp as morning dew,
Each step a wager, old and new,
A world the claw alone finds true.

He chambers rounds against the dark,
His thumb at steel, his mind she gnaws
Her eyes ignite, and leave their mark
In all his sight, in flush and calm.

Oh Lord of circles, backward run,
What ends when neither one has won?

III

They meet on a ridge split by flashing light,
The beast, a coiled burning living seam;
The mountain frozen, stretched to white,
Their gaze a scripture, rimmed in dream.

He lifts the gun. The leopard stays—
A god, a sister, none, or both—
And in that stare, the old malaise
Is loosed. He drops the gun, his oath
Undone. Her eyes, a question laid
On stone and snow, refuse the claim.

Steel lowered, mountain heartbeat played
Whispers private, a not-quite-human name.

He leaves the wild, the wild remains,
Two shadows lost in parting strains.

Economic Decay Triptych

On Full Faith and Credit

- after Re(e)vela(ua)tion and the SEC

The debt is fake—we've got the bomb.
Let Nasdaq crash, let hell unpeg.
A blonde uncoils in Oklahoma...
The debt is fake! We've got the bomb.

She draws our flag with lipstick balm,
a drone films her from mountain ledge.
The debt is fake! We've got the bomb.
Let Nasdaq crash, let hell unpeg.

Yield Curve(y)

- with mallwalkers and PAWGs

What's real is yield, and she is fair.
She walks the mall in just a thong.
Behind her trails a talking bear—
what's real is Yield, and Yield is fair.

The fountain screams. The air smells spare.
Yield says: "my song is a Revenue Song."
What's real is yield, and she was fair.
She walks the mall in just a thong.

Divine Deterrent

- for a girl spinning in broadcast snow

God won't foreclose if breasts are bare
and angels orbit ICBMs.
Texas girls know what's not there!
God won't foreclose if breasts are bare.

She mouths the pledge with vacant stare.
Her silence tallies market whims,
and angels orbit ICBMs.
God won't foreclose if breasts are bare.

Maybe I'm Not a Poet

Thank you for fixing our
   planter box,
reads the sign I notice,
   lying sideways,
pushed over,
as I stop
to light a cigarette.

And I thought
on kindnesses,
both received
and unseen,
and they all became
indistinguishable.

Inscrutable
to meet, in the wild,
a meaning of our.

Désir

Op. IV

Monody in B Minor

It was Grandfather's watch and when Father gave it to me he said I give you the mausoleum of all hope and desire.

— William Faulkner

Desire, though—desire is true sensuality. You woke up together, maybe. You know how when people sleep together often enough their hearts start to sync, not exactly *ba-dum ba-dum* but more like *babadum-dum*—off, human, a little drunk. It's a song, not a gong. Desire is what happens when you wake up together and your hearts and your hangovers are both doing that.

Desire can last. It lives with smells and rough skin. Desire arrives knowing Obsession was a joke.

"None of this matters after you meet each other," my friend said, but he says *nunns'dis matters* to everything. "A Sensualist is not merely a hedonist," says Anna Krivolapova:

> A Sensualist is a man who is sentimental to the point of wickedness, a sanguine melancholy that becomes its own weather system. Pleasure, joy, and rage ferment inside his chest, to a level that can only be tempered with Education.

I like that. Desire is Obsession educated by Ruin. I don't know if I've ever felt true desire.

Lilies of the Morning

When each morning comes
Aurora walks barefoot through the valley
snaring her dress on every thorn

In her train,

All the lilies wrench at once,
rending downward into Earth,
tearing skyward at the Air,
uncurling white tongues.

Song for the Stranger

Oh you who wander, I greet you with palms open!
Step down from your steed, set boots in grass and dew.
Let rise your breath with the starlight;
Shoulders dipped in smoke and cloud.
See how the night throws its great drape over the fields?
I call to you, yes, you, to you!

Riding there, body ghosted in lamplight.
Stride toward the high, unspeaking calling.
Harvest what the day's hand has sown.
Let the coins of now gleam in your satchel,
contented with bread, contented with darkness,
singing away the old world's blame.

Wander the shining, sunlit road,
where the high cliffs become blue mist.
Dress your soul in the dress of forgiveness,
let your faith pulse like clean cool air—
You stranger I see, moving always between light and shade.

Spring Question

Fresh news ending a cold spring
  reviving parched lips

Mountain for a house
(I have made)
animals for friends
  wind and sorrow
companions on the stone

While joy endures
  no shade lasts.

Swords will be praised
  by those who have bled.

Mausoleum thistles
  flowering sands of time
  learn by walking
  endure a length of waiting

Three days:
  hoping
  waiting
  leaving

Patience I choose—
drink from rain in barrels
smell the roses pass,
do not pluck

Wisdom
grows in the old;
etched, branched limbs
blows in rainburst
entombs in dust
scorched by Time

Letter Lost

From gold I have gathered
only the strain of striving.
I staked my future
untied my rope and slipped away.

Now I wait in patience,
put no faith in Fortune,
plant no roots in borrowed shade.
A stranger's share is all I find,
my fate lost like a letter never sent.

I've cried out to the Sun;
who turned away,
knowing not my face.

Where is my companion,
the one who knows the path?
Perhaps my voice will drift
to him across this field.

Graveyard Lesson

This world–
  shelter for the stranger,
  not for the dweller.

Other days:
  hope,
  vigil,
  arrival.

Oh soul–
  how long in sleep?
  how long numb to the wind of your fate?

Listen:
  to those who have walked far,
  to the old who know the crossways.

What I have gathered–
  years of knowledge, years of sorrow;
  before their stony sepulchres,
    reading silent lessons
    of those gone before.

Comfort Is Plenty

I

Clarity speaks in doubt;
truthful men are scarce.
Where is the wise one?
My loyal,
brother who holds fast?

Flicker in the dark, cast light
upon bodies without weight.

Sadness settles in; I wait and wait.
My youth is gone,
hope burned down to ember.

II

Some stand near but drift far as fog.
Some hearts only open
when the weather turns.

A true friend appears in trouble;
loyalty is thinnest
when comfort is plenty.

Faithful ones fade,
longing aches under all this sky.

III

Only blackbirds listen
to what I can't bear to tell.
Patience grows the taste
of iron and ash.

How long, heart,
will you hold this burden?
When will sorrow set down its
load
on the road ahead?

Kindness Returns Downriver

No longer for you the sunwild plain,
nor the bottomless guilt of absence,
choose now channels where shadows gurgle over root,
playing their songs on stone.
Cut loose the anchor!
May strong current teach you rest.
Run freely in the blackdrift.
Doubt is but sand and wind.

Patience.
It is the slow swirl under cypress knees.
Turn from envy—its teeth gnaw at the nerves.
Let sorrow's ripples pass.
Speak only what the cattails know.
Smile as the water closes round a stone.

Forgive the stumbles of those moving through the reeds
come back to kindness as river returns to mouths.
Let longing stand in the low mist,
forget wrongs, noble-hearted,
as the heron forgets the snare,
lifting into the pale margin of morning.

Chiaroscuro

Past the reach of your fire, knowledge sleeps,
cool in the half-dark, patience sifting tangled roots.
Trouble and peace coil together like smoke and dawn.
Hunt your supper in the shadow of the sycamore,
curse not the rising silt when it stains your boots.
Want only what half-blooms in shade and sun.
Let your call drift, neither whispered nor shouted.
Forgiveness beads on the leaf, waiting for the wind.

Companions in heart! Let patience rend your days
when the bitch of luck flees and hunger tugs.
All is washed away—moondark blurs to riverlight.
Desire dissipates, shallow friends recede.
Wisdom's shade walks before you on the bank.
See how the World, candle-lit and clouded,
turns and glances away, shadowed in mystery.
Keep wrapt your scars, as fox pups in the canebrake.

Walk upright, shadow-draped, humility your shield.
Move quiet through places where sunlight doesn't pool,
and journey on, starlit, as silence closes 'round behind
you.

To the Sea

(From Canto Novo by Gabriele d'Aunnzio)

I

To the sea, to the sea, my dear, come, be near
my free, green Adriatic, fragrant, clear,
sad as a song and sacred to the now,
to the poets' sea, whose salt has touched my brow.
From the rocks, look—fresh and bright,
Juno's dawn emerges, sharp with light.
A shiver of silver stirs the sea,
and the flowering woods sing to the wind.
Zephyrus sings his wedding songs.
My dear, you hear? From porch and wall,
through every vein the sap ascends,
a warm, invading conqueror bends.

II

See how, from every alder's shade,
the joy of greenness rises free
and lifts toward dawn in leaf and blade.
Don't you hear their ecstasy?
Don't you hear the songs that rise,
voluptuous on rosy tides?
Don't you stretch forth your arms in praise
to take the gifts our hands provide?

III

Oh my dear, timid in your ways,
you offer from your quiet grace
from hills of opal, lakes serene.
The violets lift a yearning face
bloom toward sunlight's golden sheen.
Smile, Oh sun. Not even the god
who fills our veins with holy fire
can veil your blaze. We are the rod,
the virgin shoots of pure desire,
sprouting from fertile boughs anew.
Smile, Oh my sea, smile once again,
with love and glory shining through.
A bride to you, tonight, I bring.

Acknowledgements

I owe particular thanks to Anna Krivolapova, who, through insistence rather than encouragement, made publication unavoidable at a moment when avoidance would have been easier. Tom Will must be thanked as well, for being better than me, and *always* being around to talk *poesy*. I am also grateful to Peter Guitl and the rest of the crew at *Frontier Magazine* for first publishing *Ruin's* "Apologia", "The Festival Is Over", and "Not Orpheus, I", and for carrying those poems far beyond their New Orleans birthplace. Additionally, the priceless editrix of *Spectra*, Erica Avey, was kind enough to let me debut "Quartet For Two" in her journal.

I have also to thank the readers who continued to show up for History, and who stuck with me while poem after poem was workshopped, revised, discarded, and tried again. My sole condition for publishing this first book was that I remain responsible for every aspect of it that could be brought under my control; accordingly, any errors, mechanical or curatorial, are mine entirely.

This book was set in Source Serif 4, with headings and ornaments in IM Fell English SC.

It was typeset in LuaLaTeX from a unified source, without reflow or template substitution.

The page is 5.5 by 8.5 inches.

Printed and bound in the United States.

This edition was designed and prepared by the author for St. Expedite Press.

No algorithms were granted editorial authority.

www.ingramcontent.com/pod-product-compliance
Lightning Source LLC
LaVergne TN
LVHW090536110826
845146LV00003B/1133

* 9 7 9 8 9 9 4 2 0 3 5 0 7 *